Quotes for Personal Excellence – 7

Time

One Hundred Quotes and Thoughts
with One Hundred Insightful Illustrations of Lord Ganesha

R.N. Kogata • Lalita Kogata

DK PRINTWORLD
Publishers of Indian Traditions

First Published in India, 2015
ISBN 13: 978-81-246-0759-6
ISBN 10: 81-246-0759-1

A creation of:
Mr R.N. Kogata and Mrs Lalita Kogata
608, Hiran Magari, Sector - 11, Udaipur, India
Phones: +91-94141 58870, +91-294-258 3870
devkush@rediffmail.com

Printed and published by:
D.K. Printworld (P) Ltd.
'Vedasri', F-395, Sudarshan Park
(Metro Station: Ramesh Nagar), New Delhi - 110 015
Phones: 011-2545 3975 / 2546 6019   Fax: 011-2546 5926
e-mail: indology@dkprintworld.com   Web: www.dkprintworld.com

Preface

Time is said to be eternal. It is said that it has neither a beginning nor an end. Yet we are able to measure it as years, months, weeks, days, hours, minutes and seconds and have also given meaning to past, present and future.

Time has great meaning. It exists always. Time moves. It never stops. Time is fleeting. It is changing. Time is a free force. It does not wait for any one. Time is precious. Time is money. It is one of the most powerful factor in human life. A minute not usefully spent is an eternal loss. Time once lost is lost forever. It can never be regained. It can never be captured. Therefore it is the most potent factor. Even the strongest and powerful monarchs have been helpless before time. Even they could not command time to stop. Everything in this world is commanded and decided by time. It conquers all. Nobody can escape the hold of time. It is the time which gives us the opportunity to make use of it. Those who make best use of time and avail those opportunities grow and rise in life. Those who waste their time lag behind. They fail to make any mark in life. He is the wisest who makes the best use of time. He rises to the great heights who keeps pace with the time. It influences every single moment and everything we do. Managing time is managing life.

The entire creation moves on according to a time pattern. Our life is measured in terms of time. We grow in time, live in time and perish in time. There is time for everything. There is time to be born, to die, to plant, to pluck up which is planted; Time to kill, to heal, to break down and to build up; Time to weep, to laugh, to mourn and to dance; Time to embrace and time to refrain from embracing; Time to get, to lose, to keep and to cast away; Time to rend, to sew, to keep silence and to speak; Time to love, to hate, for war and for peace. But the time is limited, so don't waste it living someone else's life. The time flies and never returns. If you waste time, it wastes you. Killing time is not a murder; it is a suicide. Those who do not know the importance of time, waste it or rather they spend it doing nothing. It means, by wasting time one is not harming others but harming himself. Ordinary people merely go on thinking how to spend their time. The wise and talented make use of it fruitfully.

"A stitch in time saves nine" is a popular idiom. It means that an act done in time saves from inconvenience and troubles. It brings reward. It is gainful and it saves one from hassles and confusions. Unnecessary delay and lazy attitude towards one's assigned duty is very dangerous. The great men of the world rose to fame, glory and success because they always made best use of their time. They made a mark in time. They became immortal. They are guides and sources of inspiration for generations to come.

'Time is the best medicine', it is said that time heals all wounds and it even heals what reason cannot. All human beings are emotional. When negative emotions like fear, anger, envy and jealousy overtake a person, he loses reason and acts in haste leading to serious consequences. He may repent later, as emotions cool down. But the damage done is done and remains forever. Even that damage can also be healed with the passage of time. People involved may forget and forgive. That is the speciality of time and its healing touch.

Time is also said to be a wise counsellor. Passage of time allows an individual to grow. This growth gives experience. Experience helps in decision making. Time reminds one to act and to act wisely. The wisest makes use of the time fruitfully and grieves the most at the loss of time.

To ensure best use of time in life, one needs to be very punctual. Punctuality avoids inconvenience and tension. It offers great opportunity, which, if struck properly brings out wonderful results. Opportunity once lost is hardly regained. Proper use of time brings success and achievements. Doing everything in time should be the guiding principle of life. Some people always complain that there is no time for them to do anything. That is not correct. If one wisely plans his activities, there will be time for everything happening in life. Man cannot say that he has nothing of his own. Time which is valuable is all his own. Let us learn to use our time fruitfully. This is the key to success. So, we should understand the importance of time and live a purposeful life. We should make maximum use of each and every moment. It should be valued. We are successful in life only when we make the best use of time.

It should be realized that we should have time for the loved ones, for dreams, for faith, for education, for a worthy cause, for leisure, for earning money, for nature and so on and one should balance and manage his time for its best use. We all know that we can optimize the use of time by prioritizing, organizing, setting clear goals, breaking goals down into discrete steps, identifying areas of wastage of time, reviewing progress and avoiding procrastination. But many of us still do not give its due importance to time.

Therefore we have conceived the idea of this book to tell you much more on time in just few hours. These meaningful quotes about time will touch, inspire and move you and you can thus endeavour to be the master of your own destiny.

This book is having 100 carefully chosen quotations on Time, mixed, modified or created. Some of the thoughts presented are ours and others are from the people who have stood by and worked for the values, some were famous names and some others were ordinary people. We have tried to indicate in the acknowledgement page name of the persons who have been quoted wherever we could remember. Our sincere thanks to all these great personalities and eminent writers, who have given such invaluable thoughts to this world. Any amendment / addition in this regard is most welcome from the readers.

Ganesha gives peace, prosperity and wisdom also and therefore, each of the quotes in this book has a painting of Lord Ganesha to inspire you. These paintings have been created by our professional artists keeping in view the theme of every quote.

We prostrate before our parents Smt Kanchan Devi & Shri Bhairav Lal Kogata, and late Kamla Devi Nuwal and late Prof. K.M. Nuwal, whose blessings have enabled us to grow in life.

With the expectation of blessings and constructive feedback from all of you.

Lalita & R.N. Kogta

Time

One Hundred Quotes and Thoughts
with One Hundred Insightful Illustrations of Lord Ganesha

Acknowledgement

Quotations from some eminent writers, philosophers and great personalities have been included in this book. Details of the same are given below. We sincerely thank all of them.

Page No.	Quotation by	Page No.	Quotation by	Page No.	Quotation by
T-1	Charles Darwin	T-32	John Thornton	T-65	Marcus Aurelius
T-2	Baltasar Gracian	T-33	Charles Caleb Colton	T-67	Denis Waitley
T-3	Karen Lamb	T-34	Richard H. Nelson	T-68	John Randolph
T-4	Baltasar Gracian	T-35	Auguste Rodin	T-69	Harvey Mackay
T-5	Margaret Bonnano	T-36	Mark Victor Hansen	T-70	Jim Rohn
T-7	Samuel Butler	T-37	Sergei Lukyanenko	T-71	Jawaharlal Nehru
T-8	Charles Richards	T-38	Thomas Sowell	T-72	Herbert Spencer
T-11	Coco Chanel	T-39	Sparky Anderson	T-74	Carl Sandburg
T-12	Lord Chesterfield	T-40	Sara Paddison	T-75	Denis Waitley
T-13	Brooke Shields	T-43	St Francis of Assisi	T-76	Thomas Edison
T-14	Will Rogers	T-44	Andrew Jackson	T-77	Henry van Dyke
T-15	Johann Wolfgang	T-45	Michael Althsuler	T-78	William Penn
T-16	Colin Powell	T-46	Shoppenhauer	T-79	Chanakya
T-17	Dr Seuss	T-47	C.S. Lewis	T-80	Ivan Turgenev
T-18	Zall	T-48	Franklin Field	T-81	Leonardo da Vinci
T-20	Benjamin Franklin	T-49	William Butler Yeats	T-82	Charles Caleb Colton
T-21	Lewis F. Korns	T-50	Stephen R. Covey	T-83	Charles Caleb Colton
T-22	Benjamin Franklin	T-51	Henry David Thoreau	T-84	Leonard Bernstein
T-23	Elbert Hubbard	T-52	Leo Kennedy	T-90	Michael LeBoeuf
T-24	Anthony D'Angelo	T-53	Martin Luther King, Jr.	T-91	Jeremy Irons
T-25	Sir John Lubbock	T-54	Judge Judy	T-92	Alice Bloch
T-26	Peter Turla	T-55	Adlai E. Stevenson	T-93	Arnold Bennett
T-27	Elisabeth Kubler	T-56	Marcel Proust	T-95	Art Buchwald
T-28	Henry Wadsworth	T-58	Ralph Waldo Emerson	T-97	Ralph Waldo Emerson
T-29	Stacey Charter	T-59	Jean de la Bruyère	T-98	Benjamin Franklin
T-30	Samuel Smiles	T-60	Alan Lakein	T-99	Charles Buxton
T-31	Wellins Calcott	T-61	Denis Waitley	T-100	Brian Tracy

A man,
who dares to waste
an hour,
has not discovered
the value of life.

A wise person
does at once,
what a fool does at last.

Both do the same thing;
but at different times.

A year from now
you will wish
you had started today.

All that
really belongs to us
is time;

even he
who has
nothing else
has that.

Being rich is
having money;

being wealthy is
having time.

Better late than never
is a meaningless consolation
for a man who has
lost the opportunity
of a lifetime.

Do not be anxious about tomorrow,
for tomorrow will be anxious for itself.

Let the day's own challenges
be sufficient for the day.

Do not be fooled by the calendar.

There are only
as many days in the year
as you make use of.

One man gets
only a week's value
out of a year
while another man gets
a full year's value
out of a week.

Do not count
every hour in the day,

make every hour
in the day count.

Do not say
that you do not have
enough time.

You have exactly the same
number of hours per day
that were given to
Mother Teresa, Albert Einstein,
and Mahatma Gandhi.

Do not spend time
beating on a wall,
hoping to transform it
into a door.

Do not waste a minute
not being happy.

If one window closes,
run to the next window
or break down a door.

Do not watch the clock;
do what it does.

Keep going.

Even if you are on the
right track,
you will get run over
if you just sit there.

Every second is
of infinite value.

Nothing is precious
than this day.

Have fun in your command.

Don't always run at a breakneck pace.

Take leave when you've earned it:
Spend time with your family.

How
did
it
get
so late
so soon?

T-17

How long a minute is?
It depends on which side
of the bathroom door
you are on.

If we spend our time
with regrets of yesterday,
and worries about what
might happen tomorrow,
we have no today to live.

If you have time,

don't wait for time.

If you keep yourself busy
looking at time,

you will not know
that it is passing away.

If you love life,
then don't squander time,
for that's the stuff
life is made of.

If you want the work
well done,
select a busy man;

the other kind has no
time.

In order to succeed
you must fail,

so that you know
what not to do
next time.

In reality,
people can make time
for what they choose to do;

it is not really the time
but the will that is lacking.

It is better to do
the right thing slowly
than the wrong thing quickly.

It is only when we know
we have a limited time
on earth and that
we have no way of knowing
when is our time up,

we will begin to live
each day to the fullest,
as if it was
the only day we had.

It takes less time
to do a thing right

than

to explain
why you did it wrong.

Life is all about timing . . .
the unreachable becomes reachable,
the unavailable becomes available,
the unattainable . . . attainable.

Have patience,
wait it out

as it's all about timing.

Lost wealth
may be reclaimed
by industry,
lost knowledge by serious study,
lost health by temperance or medicine,

but lost time is gone forever.

Make good use of time …
reflect that

yesterday cannot be recalled,
tomorrow cannot be assured,
today is only yours,

you will be a big loser
if you procrastinate it.

Men have invented instruments
to measure the motion of time,

but they have no scales to weigh,
no figures to compute,
no words to describe its value.

Much may be done
in those little shreds
and patches of time
that every day produces,
which most men
throw away.

Never let yesterday
use up today.

Nothing is a waste of time
if you utilize the experience wisely.

NOW is the only time there is.

Make your NOW wow,
your minutes miracles,
and your days pay.

Your life will have
magnificently lived
and invested,
and when you die
you will have
made a difference.

T-36

One day you will hear
the sound of time
rustling as sand slips
through
your fingers like.

People who have time
will inevitably waste
the time of people
who have work to do.

People who live in the past
generally are afraid
to compete in the present.

I've my faults,
but living in the past
is not one of them.

There's no future in it.

Realize that
now in this moment of time,
you are creating.

You are creating
your next moment.

That is what is real.

Remember the past,
plan for the future,
but live for today,

because
yesterday is gone and
tomorrow may never come.

Speed Limit
of Time:
One moment at a time.

Start by doing
what is necessary,
then what is possible,

and suddenly
you are doing the impossible.

Take time to deliberate;

but when the time
for action arrives,
stop thinking and go in.

The bad news is
time flies.

The good news is
you are the pilot.

The common man
is not concerned
about the
passage of time.

The man of talent
is driven by it.

The future is something
which everyone reaches
at the rate of sixty minutes an hour,
whatever he does, whoever he is.

The great dividing line between
success and failure
can be expressed
in five words:

I did not have time.

The innocent and the beautiful
have no enemy but time.

The key is not
in spending time,
but
in investing it.

The meeting of two eternities,
the past and future . . .

is precisely
the present moment.

The surest way to be late
is to have plenty of time.

The time is always right
to do what is right.

T-53

The time to change
was yesterday;

the time to wake up
is now.

The time
to stop a revolution
is at the beginning,

not at the end.

The time we have
at our disposal
every day
is elastic;

the passions we feel expand it,
those that we inspire contract it
and habit fills up what remains.

This is the beginning of a new day.
God has given me this day to use as I will.
I can waste it or use it for good.
What I do today is important, because

I am exchanging a day of my life for it.
When tomorrow comes,
this day will be gone forever,
leaving in its place something
that I have traded for it.

I want it to be a gain, not a loss;
good, not evil; success, not failure;
in order that I shall not regret
the price I paid for it.

This time,
like all times,
is a very good one,

if we but know
what to do with it.

T-58

Those who make
the worse use of time

are the first to complain
of its shortness.

Time = Life.

Therefore,
waste your time
and waste your life,

or master your time
and master your life.

Time and health
are two precious assets
that we don't recognize
and appreciate
until they have been depleted.

Time invested in improving ourselves cuts down on time wasted in disapproving others.

T-62

Time is a circus,
always packing up
and moving away.

So don't forget to enjoy it,
when it is available.

Time is a gift . . .

that's why
now is called "the present".

T-64

Time is a sort of river of passing events,
and strong is its current;

no sooner is a thing brought to sight
than it is swept by
and another takes its place
and this too
will be swept away.

Time is an asset.

To be managed more carefully
than money.

Try to spend it
with the people
who share your dreams,
desire and destiny.

Time is an equal opportunity employer.

Each human being has exactly the same number of
hours and minutes every day.
Rich people can't buy more hours.
Scientists can't invent new minutes.
And you can't save time to spend it on another day.

Even so, time is amazingly fair and forgiving.
No matter how much time you've wasted in the past,
you still have an entire tomorrow.

Time is at once
the most valuable
and the most perishable
of all our possessions.

Time is free, but it's priceless.

You can't own it, but you can use it.

You can't keep it, but you can spend it.

Once you've lost it,

You can never get it back.

Time is more valuable than money.

You can get more money,
but you cannot get more time.

Time is not measured
by the passing of years
but by what one does,
what one feels,
and what one achieves.

Time is one thing that
man is always trying to kill,

but it in turn kills him.

T-72

Time is precious;
even an inch of gold
can't buy an inch of time.

Time is the coin of your life.

It is the only coin you have,
and only you can determine
how it will be spent.

Be careful in allowing
other people spend it for you.

T-74

Time is the most precious element of human existence.

A successful person knows how to put energy into time and how to draw success from it.

Time is the only capital
that a person has,
and the only thing
he can't afford to lose.

Time is too slow for those who wait,
too swift for those who fear,
too long for those who grieve,
too short for those who rejoice,
but for those who love,
time is eternity.

Time is what we want most,
but what we use worst.

Time perfects men
and
destroys them as well.

T-79

Time sometimes flies like a bird,
sometimes crawls like a snail;

but a man is happiest when
he does not even notice
whether it passes
swiftly or slowly.

Time stays long enough
for anyone who uses it.

T-81

Time, the cradle of hope . . .

Wisdom walks before it, opportunity with it,
and repentance behind it.

He who has made it his friend
will have little to fear from his enemies,
but he who has made it his enemy
will have little to hope from his friends.

Time . . . advances like
a slow tide,
but retreats like
a swift torrent.

To achieve great things,
two things are needed:

a plan and
not quite enough time.

T-84

To get through
the hardest journey
we need take only
one step at a time,

but we must keep on stepping.

To kill time,
a committee meeting
is a perfect weapon.

It took only a moment
to cause this head to fall,
and a hundred years will not
suffice to produce its like.

T-86

Tough times get you real friends,
others get you tough times.

T-87

Treasure every moment that you have
and treasure it more because
you shared it with someone special,
special enough to spend your time with.

And remember time waits for no one.

Unless you value yourself,
you will not value your time.

Until you value your time,
you will not do anything with it.

Waste your money
and you are only
out of money,

but waste your time
and you have lost
a part of your life.

We all have our time machines.

Some take us back,
they're called memories.

Some take us forward,
they're called dreams.

We say we waste time,
but that is impossible.

We waste ourselves.

We shall never have more time.

We have, and always had,
all the time there is.

No object is served in waiting
until next week or even until tomorrow.

Keep going . . .
Concentrate on something useful.

What may be done
at any time
will be done
at no time.

Whether it is the best of times
or the worst of times,

it is the only time we have got.

T-95

Yesterday is a cancelled cheque,
tomorrow is a promissory note,
today is
the only cash you have;

spend it wisely.

You cannot do
a kindness too soon;

for you never know
how soon it will be too late.

You may delay,
but time will not.

T-98

You will never find
time for anything.

If you want time
you must make it.

Your greatest resource
is your time.

T-100